DISCIPLES YOKES

For Growing Christians

Chuck Winters

WESTBOW
PRESS®

A DIVISION OF THOMAS NELSON
& ZONDERVAN

WestBow Press books may be ordered through booksellers or by contacting:

WestBow Press
A Division of Thomas Nelson & Zondervan
1663 Liberty Drive
Bloomington, IN 47403
www.westbowpress.com
1 (866) 928-1240

ISBN: 978-1-9736-9652-0 (sc)
ISBN: 978-1-9736-9651-3 (e)

Library of Congress Control Number: 2020913433

Print information available on the last page.

WestBow Press rev. date: 08/07/2020

FOR THE BURDENED AND HEAVY HEARTED

Take a journey with us into the life you have longed to live. Find the power and freedom of the Holy Spirit working mightily in and through your life. Discover what it means to be a **Disciple** of Jesus Christ. Delight in the quality of life that Jesus called **Abundant Life**! Please join us in a simple approach to having our lives transformed into the very nature of Jesus our Lord.

Please allow me to share a few vital word meanings for this journey.

1) **DISCIPLE:** A person who is developing the character of Jesus Christ, Yah Shua, into his or her life.
2) **YAH SHUA:** **Jesus** is the Greek name for our Lord's Hebrew name, **Yah Shua**. For the purposes of this study we will be using our Lord's spoken name, Yah Shua, which is the name He was called while in human form on earth. Yah Shua means **Yahweh Saves**! (Yahweh is God's personal name and is sometimes referred to as Jehovah.)
3) **YOKE:** A wooden beam that linked two animals of burden together and enabled them to pull together. This made their workload easier. When we put ourselves in Yah Shua's Yoke, our Lord carries the burden of the load for us!

Opening Prayer:

Dear Father,
Please help me to become the disciple of Jesus that I long to be in my heart. I commit to You that I will do all I can to achieve the goal of becoming like Christ.

Signed; _____

Date, _____

Just for your record please fill in the following things:

*The one thing you worry about the most.

*The one thing you fear the most.

*What makes you angry the quickest?

What is a disciple?

What does Yah Shua mean? How does His name apply to your life?

What things are you currently yoked to in your life?

4) **HUMAN NATURE'S DESIRE:** Our fallen nature's way of responding to problems and circumstances in life. This is the result of the sin of Adam and Eve in the Garden of Eden and has been handed down to all humans.

Read the following verses and think about what God is saying about how prevalent sin is in the human nature.

Romans 5:12
When Adam sinned, sin entered the entire human race. Adam's sin brought death, so death spread to everyone, for everyone sinned. (NLT)

Psalm 14:3
But no, all have turned away from God; all have become corrupt. No one does good, not even one! (NLT)

5) **LEGALISM:** When a person attempts to please God by doing things.

According to the following verse how successful could we ever be in pleasing God in our own **self-effort**?

Isaiah 64:6
We are all infected and impure with sin. When we proudly display our righteous deeds, we find they are but filthy rags. Like autumn leaves, we wither and fall. And our sins, like the wind, sweep us away. (NLT)

6) **YOKEFELLOW:** A person who mentors with us as an accountability partner. (On page 15 you will find a detailed outline of the responsibilities of the Yokefellow.)

Daily Prayer:

Dear Father,
Show me today the truth about my own human nature. Give me the grace to come to the place in my life that I will no longer compare myself to any other standard than You.

What does the term <u>human nature</u> mean to you?

How difficult is it for you to resist temptation in your life?

How do we go about becoming pleasing to God? (Circle one)

a) Always be nice.
b) Go to church
c) Give a lot of money
d) Accept Yah Shua

> **Put into your own words what you believe the fallen human nature is like according to Isaiah 64:6.**

A LIFE TRANSFORMATION

In Matthew's account of the Good News, Yah Shua our Messiah gives us our primary purpose for living,

Matthew 28:18-20
Jesus came and told his disciples, "I have been given complete authority in heaven and on earth. Therefore, go and <u>make disciples</u> of all the nations, baptizing them in the name of the Father and the Son and the Holy Spirit. <u>Teach</u> these new disciples to obey all the commands I have given you. And be sure of this: I am with you always, even to the end of the age." (NLT)

When we become Christians, our lives start a dramatic time of change. We are a **Believer** the moment we accept Christ into our hearts. We become a **Disciple of Christ** as we learn to live a life of truth. This new life doesn't come just through accumulating mental facts, but in acquiring the **character** of Yah Shua.

Consider what Paul says to the Church in Rome about the need to have a dramatic change in one's entire life after coming to Christ for salvation.

Romans 12:2
Don't copy the behavior and customs of this world, but let God transform you into a new person by changing the way you think. (NLT)

This **New Person** Paul is talking about is Christ's nature living in our lives!

Daily Prayer:

Dear Father,
Help me to understand the wonder and glory that comes by being transformed into a brand new person by the power of Your Holy Spirit.

What Christian activities have more priority today than <u>making disciples</u> in your life?

What do you think about this statement?
"We are not mature disciples of Yah Shua until we are reproducing ourselves as disciples!"

In what ways could you say today that your life has been transformed by the power of God?

Take a few minutes to memorize Romans 12:2, and write it in this space.

What would prevent a Christian from being transformed into the character of Christ?

Paul instructs the church at Ephesus with the following urgent plea:

Ephesians 4:21-24

21. Since you have heard all about him and have learned the truth that is in Jesus,

22. Throw off your <u>old evil nature</u> and your former way of life, which is rotten through and through, full of lust and deception.

23. Instead, there must be a spiritual renewal of your thoughts and attitudes.

24. You must <u>display a new nature</u> because you are a new person, created in God's likeness--righteous, holy, and true. (NLT)

If we don't have Christ's character fused into our lives, we will find ourselves trying to follow a great number of rules and regulations in order to be a **follower** of Yah Shua. This turns into another form of **legalism**, and will always leave us frustrated and defeated as Yah Shua's followers. Eventually we find ourselves worn out spiritually because we will inevitably discover that we are trying to follow Yah Shua in the power of our own self-effort! I think we have all discovered that our **self-effort** at accomplishing spiritual vitality always ends in defeat! I would like to invite you to join me in a different journey, a journey toward being transformed to Christ's character first, then allowing that character within to direct our actions as God's Holy Spirit so pleases!

When Yah Shua was born of the Virgin Mary in Bethlehem, it was a great miracle. For God to become man was never anticipated by humanity.

Now, for Yah Shua to live in our hearts is no less a miracle, and this miracle was never anticipated! The great thing is that we get to participate with God Himself in this miracle!

Daily Prayer:

Dear Father,
Help me this day to see my human nature in the light and truth of Your Word.

Have you ever started in a discipleship-training program and ended up feeling frustrated?

Have you ever finished a discipleship training method and then found a few months later that you were not applying the things you learned?

In Ephesians 4:24, what is the force that creates God's likeness into our lives?

Would you record a prayer asking God to create Christ's likeness into your life?

BEARING A YOKE THAT LIGHTENS THE LOAD

In Matthew 11:28-30, we find the only place in the gospels where Yah Shua actually gives us a picture of His personal character, in His own words. Very telling indeed! These are the bedrock character traits of Yah Shua Himself, given by Him, which formed the greatness of the person He was, and is! Please pay careful attention to His words!

Matthew 11:28-30
Then Jesus said, "Come to me, all of you who are weary and carry heavy burdens, and I will give you rest. Take my yoke upon you. Let me teach you, because <u>I am humble and gentle</u>, and you will find rest for your souls. For my yoke fits perfectly, and the burden I give you is light." (NLT)

When Yah Shua says, "Let me teach you," He uses the same word used in Matthew 28 when He commands us to make **disciples** or to **teach** all nations! Yah Shua did not teach His followers how to do a Bible study, or how to witness, or how to have a quiet time. He did teach them about His **character!** The Christian skills of witnessing, Bible study, quiet time, and a host of others are all important, but we find that developing Christ's character is the first step that needs to be taken before other skills are developed. We might say that one has to get to first base before going on to second base! Yah Shua referred to learning His character as a **yoke.** We are going to refer to learning about Yah Shua's character as **Yah Shua Yokes** or **Disciple Yokes.** We are going to trust the truthfulness of God's word that this journey will not be difficult, but instead this journey will **fit us perfectly** and will actually lighten our heavy loads! This is because Yah Shua carries the major burden of our heavy loads as we take on His yoke.

Daily Prayer:

Dear Father,
Help me this day to identify the things in my life, which are not pleasing to You.

What is it in Matthew 11:28-30 that Jesus wants to teach us?

What are the two character traits that Jesus identifies as His own?

Would you say that these two qualities accurately describe your life today?

What does Jesus mean by finding <u>rest</u> in our lives?

How much would you be willing to give to have this <u>inner peace</u>?

PUTTING ON YAH SHUA'S YOKE

Now, the next question we have to deal with is **HOW** do we get Yah Shua's Yokes into our lives? For example, do we just decide one day to be happy? Can I say it is as simple as making a choice to be happy? I think we need a little more help than that, **we need God's help!** This is where we have to learn to **TRUST** God to help us do what we cannot do ourselves. We are going to be using the great Biblical word **TRUST**, to form an acrostic that we have seen open hearts and lives to the transforming power of God in converting our lives to the yoke of Christ's nature. The acrostic will look like this:

- **T.** The letter **T** is for Testing.
- **R.** The letter **R** is for Repent.
- **U.** The letter **U** is for Understanding.
- **S.** The letter **S** is for Sanctify.
- **T.** The last letter **T** is for Triumph.

Please take the time today to memorize this simple acrostic. It is going to become a vital part of your daily life in Christ! We are going to be learning each part of **TRUST** for the next several days.

Daily Prayer:

Dear Father,
Please help me this week to learn how to apply to my life the Yah Shua Yokes that bring glory to Your Name!

The first T in TRUST is for:

What <u>tests</u> are you going through right now?

R stands for what?

What things in your life exist that you need to <u>repent</u> of at this time?

U is for what?

How well would you say you <u>understand</u> the things God is doing in your life right now?

S stands for what?

How does God <u>sanctify</u> your life?

T the last T in TRUST is for what?

Do you wish to live in victory over trials?

TRUST

T. The letter **T** is for **Testing**. Let's consider James 1:2-4.

James 1:2-4
Dear brothers and sisters, whenever trouble comes your way, let it be an opportunity for joy. For when your faith is <u>tested,</u> your endurance has a chance to grow. So let it grow, for when your endurance is fully developed, you will be strong in character and ready for anything. (NLT)

Here is where we must begin our journey toward our great goal of becoming conformed to the image of Yah Shua. It begins with **<u>trials</u>** or **<u>testing</u>**.

Carbon is one of the most common elements in all of nature; however, when carbon is placed under pressure and heat over time a wonderful new gem is formed-a diamond! This is exactly what God allows to happen in our lives as we endure tests. The pressure of life's tests, when we yield to the Holy Spirit's working, yields the spiritual diamond of Yah Shua's character in our lives!

Consider what Jesus says in **Matthew 7:14**

But the gateway to life is small, and the road is narrow, and only a few ever find it. (NLT)

The word Jesus uses here translated **<u>narrow</u>** literally means to put under **<u>pressure</u>** or to **<u>squeeze</u>**! The road to true life in Christ is a road of tests or pressure! **<u>Expect to be tested</u>**, don't run or hide from them as that will only delay the lesson! It is far better to take on Yah Shua's Yoke now than to wait for another opportunity! Next opportunities are usually much more difficult!

Daily Prayer:

Dear Father,
Help me to see the tests and trials in my life through your eyes and to understand how you wish to use them for your glory.

Write James 1:2-4 in your own words in the following space.

How do you feel about <u>tests</u> and <u>trials</u> you face in life?

A) Ignore them.
B) Resent them.
C) Get through them.
D) Embrace them.

Can you think of a time that God allowed pressure in your life in order for you to grow in a certain area? What was the pressure and what did it produce?

R. The letter **R** is for **Repent**.

When the test(s) come, recognize that it is a test to lead you to a new <u>yoke</u> level. Recognize your human nature's desired response and **repent** immediately of it! We must learn to call what our fallen nature desires to do a sin! Some have said that Christians do not need to repent. However, the Apostle Paul writing to the church in Corinth, has this to say about the ongoing need to repent of our human nature's desired responses to the tests and temptations of life:

2 Corinthians 12:21
Yes, I am afraid that when I come, God will humble me again because of you. And I will have to grieve because many of you who sinned earlier have not <u>repented</u> of your impurity, sexual immorality, and eagerness for lustful pleasure. (NLT)

<u>Repent</u> means simply to turn. When we repent we confess to the Father our sinful nature's desired response, and then turn to Him for victory over it. Notice what John says in 1 John:

1 John 1:8-10
If we say we have no sin, we are only fooling ourselves and refusing to accept the truth. But if we <u>confess</u> our sins to him, he is faithful and just to forgive us and to cleanse us from every wrong. If we claim we have not sinned, we are calling God a liar and showing that his word has no place in our hearts. (NLT)

When we **confess**, we are in fact agreeing with God. God then promises that He will forgive us and cleanse us. Our greatest goal in life is to not only be forgiven, but to be cleansed of our fallen human nature. There is great <u>joy</u> in actually being cleansed of our fallen human nature, then being changed into Yah Shua's nature by the power of God's Holy Spirit!

Daily Prayer:

Dear Father,
Help me today to begin to see the glory of repentance in my life.

When you hear the word <u>repent</u>, what visual image comes first to your mind?

Do you think repentance is a one-time occurrence in a Christian's life or is there a need for ongoing repentance?

What does the word <u>repent</u> mean according to our study from the Bible?

What does the word <u>confess</u> mean in 1 John 1:8-10?

What value would you place on being cleansed of the fallen nature?

Another aspect of repenting of our desired way of responding is that in doing so we are actually admitting to God that we need help in overcoming the test or temptation. For some reason we seem to want to handle all our tests and temptations ourselves! The growing Christian is constantly learning that we need God's help in our lives. Acknowledging our need for the Spirit's help is not a sign of weakness, but rather the mark of a maturing disciple.

Consider this statement Paul makes to the church at Corinth:

1 Cor. 10:13
But remember that the temptations that come into your life are no different from what others experience. And God is faithful. He will keep the temptation from becoming so strong that you can't stand up against it. When you are tempted, he will show you a way out so that you will not give in to it. (NLT)

Please notice that it is God who delivers us, not we ourselves! When the test/temptation comes, **confess** our **desired response** as sinful and turn to God for His help. We are learning to TRUST Him for the victory that overcomes the world, the world of iniquity that lurks in our hearts!

As we grow in our knowledge of the continual need for turning away from our desired way of responding to tests and temptations, we actually begin to learn that repentance is not a word with negative meanings. It is actually to the **glory of God** that we are able to turn away from our way of living and acting in order to find the fullness of life that comes from experiencing Christ in us! Now we start to become salt and light in a dark world!

9

Daily Prayer:

Dear Father,
Please help me this day to see the joy of repentance in my life.

Does it embarrass you to ask for help?

When have you ever asked for help and received it to your benefit?

Why would a child of God not want to ask our Heavenly Father for help in a trying time, or a time of temptation?

What value should we place on being aware of God's presence and power to accomplish His will in our lives?

U. The next letter in **TRUST** is the letter **U. U** stands for **Understanding**. After we confess our sinful desired response and turn to the Father for help, we then begin to **thank** God in faith for the understanding about His Ways that we are going to be learning! What we typically want is understanding first, but that is not the way God works. We desire to ask why; then we say we will obey after we understand. But God requires that we obey first, then His understanding will follow our obedience.

Remember the carbon that is being formed into a diamond? The carbon has no idea that the pressure is molding it into a precious jewel. The carbon simply yields and the result is of great value! We have the added advantage of knowing that as we go through the test what God's ultimate purpose is. That is the way we should be while going through a test. Remember what our goal is? It is to be conformed to Yah Shua's nature first and foremost. Nothing in our lives is more important. Our sovereign God is working to create Yah Shua's Yoke, or Christ's character into our lives. Therefore we thank God for the **trial**, and thank Him for the **understanding** He is going to develop into our lives.

Here the scriptures begin to take on dramatically special meaning to our hearts! As we live in them, trust and believe them, they become **ours**! Scripture now becomes not just something we read because we are supposed to, but it becomes the lifeblood of our existence. We take personal possession of them and they possess our very lives.

Daily Prayer:

Dear Father,
Please help me to gain new levels of understanding You and Your ways.

Do you think it sounds strange to thank God for what you have not yet received from God?

Do you tend to expect an explanation before you are willing to follow an order or instruction?

Do you believe that God is truly and personally interested in your life?

Do you believe that God has a specific purpose for your life?

What would you say is God's top priority in your life?

Consider this promise from Proverbs chapter 2:

Proverbs 2:2-7
2 Tune your ears to wisdom, and concentrate on <u>understanding</u>.
3 Cry out for insight and <u>understanding</u>.
4 Search for them as you would for lost money or hidden treasure.
5 Then you will <u>understand</u> what it means to fear the LORD, and you will gain knowledge of God.
6 For the Lord grants wisdom! From his mouth come knowledge and <u>understanding</u>.
7 He grants a treasure of good sense to the godly. He is their shield, protecting those who walk with integrity. (NLT)

Here we see that the gaining of understanding is the vital step to knowing God. To **know** someone in the Bible is to have a close, personal, and intimate relationship with them. No growing child of God will be satisfied with just a casual knowledge of Him; we want to know Him! We want to know and understand **His ways**, for they are the issues of true life. Now our **tests** start to take on a whole new valuable meaning.

<u>Thank</u> the Father for the new depth of **<u>understanding</u>** He is revealing of Himself! Thank God for choosing you to share in His very Nature! Thank the Father that He is revealing and sharing His very heart with you! Thank the Father for the privilege of knowing that He is personally at work in your life!

Oh, the **<u>joy</u>** of His favored presence!

Daily Prayer:

Dear Father,
Please help me to know You as fully as I am able with the help of Your Holy Spirit.

How important does the writer of Proverbs think gaining understanding of God is?

What does it mean to <u>know</u> someone in the Biblical sense?

How important is it to understand why God allows us to go through trials?

If we don't understand why God allows us to go through trials what will our response to trials tend to become?

Would you decide today to make knowing God the focus of your life?

S. The next letter in TRUST is **S**, and this stands for **Sanctify**. In the process of salvation we are being sanctified or **set apart** for God's good purposes in our lives. The day we become a Christian we receive God's precious Spirit into our lives. This is just the beginning of a life-long journey toward becoming like Yah Shua in our hearts. The day we become a Christian we are like a newborn baby. What the TRUST strategy does is to give us the tools to cooperate with the ongoing work of God's Holy Spirit in our lives. This is exactly what sanctification is all about, being changed by the power of God! Of course we must be willing participants in the working of God! Consider these verses to the church at Thessolonica.

1Thess 5:23-24
And the very God of peace sanctify you wholly; and I pray God your whole spirit and soul and body be preserved blameless unto the coming of our Lord Jesus Christ. Faithful is he that calleth you, who also will do it. (KJV)

Do you understand that God is working to **sanctify** us totally? This is His goal, and we must get on board with His plan to accomplish this! What do we do to yield to the Father in this great undertaking? The key is simple, we start to **meditate** on specific verses which apply to the Yah Shua Yoke God is building into our lives! Now what is meditation? It is so simple we have often overlooked it!

Joshua 1:8
Study this Book of the Law continually. Meditate on it day and night so you may be sure to obey all that is written in it. Only then will you succeed. I command you--be strong and courageous! Do not be afraid or discouraged. For the LORD your God is with you wherever you go. (NLT)

Daily Prayer:

Dear Father,
Please help me today to understand how You work to sanctify my heart and how I can yield to what You are doing in my life.

How healthy would a newborn baby be if it refused to eat?

How long would it live?

Who does the work of sanctifying our hearts?

What attention do you normally give to the Spirit's working in your heart?

How can the Bible help in one's being sanctified?

Do you see the promise God gives concerning **meditation**? If we are committed to meditation then He will make us **successful**! Look at the start of this verse again!

Joshua 1:8
Study this Book of the Law continually. <u>Meditate</u> on it day and night so you may be sure to obey all that is written in it. Only then will you <u>succeed</u>. (NLT)

<u>Meditation</u> is simply taking the verse of scripture we are learning which deals with the Yah Shua Yoke we are sanctifying our life with, and **thinking** on it. We think on it constantly throughout the day and into the night as we fall asleep. We wake up in the morning thinking about it. The verse will encourage us, instruct us, and as we bury the verse into our minds and hearts it will change our lives! That verse will become a part of our thinking, and eventually control our response to any circumstance! We will be sanctified by the truth of His word in that area of our lives!

As a lamb chews the cud, it is ruminating or meditating on the cud. The sheep doesn't live by eating grass. The grass serves as an environment when mixed with the warmth and moisture in the lamb's mouth allows millions of single-celled protozoa to thrive and multiply and grow. It is actually the protozoa that, when swallowed, feeds the lamb! If the lamb doesn't ruminate, it will starve to death regardless of how much grass it eats! Meditation is the vital key that feeds the child of God. Through meditation we yield our minds and hearts to God's Holy Spirit in the life changing process of **sanctification**! Oh, the joys of becoming like Yah Shua in our lives. Yah Shua's Yoke fits perfectly, His burden is light!

Daily Prayer:

Dear Father,
Please help me this day to learn the key to success in life so that I might live a life of success to the Praise of Your glory.

What promise does God make concerning <u>meditation</u> in scripture?

What has been your thinking about how to judge <u>success</u> in your life?

How could it be possible to know large amounts of scripture yet not be conformed to Christ's character?

Can you see that having a lot of Bible knowledge could actually lead to pride if Christ's yokes of humility and gentleness are not first achieved?

T. The last letter in the TRUST strategy is **T**, and this **T** stands for **Triumph**! Let's look for a moment at what Paul writes to the church at Corinth.

2 Cor 10:17
As the Scriptures say, "The person who wishes to <u>boast</u> should <u>boast</u> only of what the Lord has done." (NLT)

Did you know it is all right to **boast** about what God has done? This is what we are going to do in this last step of **TRIUMPH**; we are going to triumph, or boast, about what God is doing in our lives! Now we aren't going to do this in front of a church unless God might direct us to do so as a testimony to encourage others, but we are going to do this weekly with one other person. This person will agree to be our **Yokefellow**.

Our Yokefellow will be going through the Yah Shua Yokes process with us. We won't be boasting about ourselves, but rather about the things our Father is teaching us in our lives! We will share how God is using the very things which would have discouraged and defeated us before, but now how God is using those very things to conform us to the nature of Christ!

Psalm 34:2-3
I will <u>boast</u> only in the LORD; let all who are discouraged take heart. Come, let us tell of the Lord's greatness; let us exalt his name together. (NLT)

Tomorrow we will see the Yokefellow process and begin to pray for God's leadership in joining up with our Yokefellow. It is thrilling to see the triumphant victory of one who is discovering the overcoming power of the Spirit and the Word realized in their life! Oh, the **joy** of those whose **triumph** is in the LORD!

Daily Prayer:

Dear Father,
Please help me this day to learn to triumph in what You are working in my life.

Have you ever considered the thrill of living in <u>victory</u> daily?

When do you currently see God's power at work in your life?

When was the last time you were able to boast about what God was doing in and through your life?

When was the last time you were discouraged about life?

Will you this day decide to live in Yah Shua's victory?

YOKEFELLOW GUIDE SHEET

The role of a Yokefellow is an exciting journey with a growing follower of Yah Shua the Messiah. It will be your privilege to walk with this growing believer as he or she experiences the **joy** of taking on the character of our Lord!

1) **Call or meet with your Disciple Yokes partner at least once each week.**
2) **Have a mutually set time for this ministry period.**
3) **Have your partner share what test(s) he or she is going through.**
4) **Have your partner share the Yah Shua Yoke(s) he has identified that God is building and strengthening into his character.**
5) **Have your partner share which verse he is meditating on and how it applies to the Yah Shua Yoke God is building into his life.**
6) **Have him share how God enabled him to have Yah Shua's victory in the trial.**
7) **Keep this information very confidential!**
8) **If your apprentice acknowledges failing a test, be very encouraging. Each day the sun comes up is a brand new opportunity to exhibit Christ to others!**
9) **Pray daily for your partner, especially in the areas you know God is working.**
10) **Be open and honest about the areas God is currently working in your own life.**

Daily Prayer:

Dear Father,
Help me this day to be firmly committed to joining with my Yokefellow in the transforming process of becoming like Christ in my heart. I pray this for Your glory.

My Yokefellow is:

We will share weekly at this time:

I will keep all things we share confidential unless we jointly decide to share with others for their encouragement.

Signed:

Yokefellow's signature:

> **The accountability of having a Yokefellow is vital to the success of becoming a disciple of Yah Shua!**

FINDING THE YAH SHUA YOKES

Yah Shua Yoke #1: JOY

Let's take our journey of Yah Shua Yokes disciple training from the letter the **Apostle James** gives to us. In this simple letter we find several character qualities given which ought to form the foundation of a growing Christian's life. Who better to learn from than James who was a little brother of Yah Shua in his own life? James knew Yah Shua from his earliest days and had the opportunity of seeing Yah Shua's character for many years before John the Baptist ever met him on the Jordan River banks.

James 1:2-4
Dear brothers and sisters, whenever trouble comes your way, let it be an opportunity for joy. For when your faith is tested, your endurance has a chance to grow. So let it grow, for when your endurance is fully developed, you will be strong in character and ready for anything. (NLT)

To have **joy** in your life means to have a **calm delight**. Does this sound strange; to face tests in life with a calm delight? It is no accident that James begins our training with the need for joy in our lives! Joy is the first fundamental ingredient of the Child of God. Why would I say this? Consider this passage from the Bible.

Nehemiah 8:10
And Nehemiah continued, "Go and celebrate with a feast of choice foods and sweet drinks, and share gifts of food with people who have nothing prepared. This is a sacred day before our Lord. Don't be dejected and sad, for the joy of the LORD is your strength!" (NLT)

Daily Prayer:

Dear Father,
*Please help me this day to begin discovering the **Joy** Jesus desires to give to me in my life.*

Would you say that people who know you would characterize you as a joyful person?

What do you think their first character quality thought of you would be?

Why would the Bible word for joy be defined as having a calm delight?

How can we actually face difficulties with a calm delight?

> **How would a calm delight be different than fear or dread in facing tests?**

Read yesterday's passage from Nehemiah again. The people of Israel were brokenhearted. They had just returned to Jerusalem from seventy years of captivity in Babylon. Jerusalem, their beloved city, was in ruins. The Temple of God was destroyed. Then, to make matters worse, the priests read and interpreted the Word of God, which helped the people see very clearly their sinfulness. God was just in His chastisement; they realized they had deserved every punishment they had endured. They stood weeping before the truth of God's Word.

Then Nehemiah gives to the weeping, broken congregation this startling word! Don't weep, but rather rejoice! Yes we have sinned, but Yahweh is a merciful God. His purposes are going to be carried out regardless of our failures. He has chosen us and called us to be His people, so **be filled with joy.** Then, Nehemiah, gives the importance of having joy, **it is our strength!** We might say it this way, without joy in our lives we will have no strength.

How many times do we allow ourselves to become angry, or get trapped under the dark clouds of discouragement? What strength is there in discouragement? Notice that the root word of discouragement is **courage**. Discouragement is the removal of courage. If we have no courage, we have no strength. God's Word tells us that the basis of courage is **joy**!

From the biblical word for **joy** we get the Bible word **grace**. Grace means **God's influence upon the heart.** What Child of God wants to live their life without God's influence upon their hearts? We might say it this way, without joy God will not have any influence in our hearts! That would certainly not be living a life as a follower of Yah Shua!

Daily Prayer:

Dear Father,
Please help me this day to experience Your joy in the manner You have formed me and desire for me to live.

How devastated do you imagine the children of Israel felt as they saw the condition of Jerusalem?

Have you ever had the horrible experience of seeing what you thought was going to destroy all your hopes and dreams in life?

What feelings did that time bring up in your heart and mind?

How did you deal with that event?

Has there been more than one of these events in your life?

Let's consider **Yah Shua's Yoke** of <u>joy</u> in John the Baptist's life.

John 3:29-30
The bride will go where the bridegroom is. A bridegroom's friend rejoices with him. I am the bridegroom's friend, and I am filled with <u>joy</u> at his success. He must become greater and greater, and I must become less and less. (NLT)

What a great heart John shows here. What **grace** received from the Father in heaven! To be filled with joy at ones own personal success is one thing, but to be filled with joy at the success of another is truly remarkable! Not to mention the other person's success means ones own personal decreasing in fame! Yah Shua later says that there was never a greater man born than John the Baptist. Why? Because John had joy, therefore grace, and therefore courage to fulfill his God given purpose in life. John's human life ended with his head cut off and placed on a platter. Yet his life ended as a spiritual champion!

In John 15:11, Yah Shua shares with us His intention and desire to share His joy with us. *"I have told you this so that you will be filled with my <u>joy</u>. Yes, your <u>joy</u> will overflow!"* (NLT) When does He give this teaching? Yah Shua gives this, as the cross of Calvary looms high on His horizon. As our precious Lord is now deliberately making His way toward the cross, His focus is on sharing His joy with His followers! Did Yah Shua need courage? Was this the time for discouragement and a weak heart? The most critical moment in mankind's entire existence was center stage, and the focus of our Master was on giving to us His <u>Joy</u>!

John 17:13
And now I am coming to you. I have told them many things while I was with them so they would be filled with my <u>joy</u>." (NLT)

Daily Prayer:

Dear Father,
Please help me this day to learn to develop a life time focus on Your reputation being the goal of my life.

How easy is it for you to rejoice in another person's victories?

Have you ever rejoiced when another person achieved the very thing that you longed to achieve?

Why would <u>humility</u> be required to have this kind of heart?

How could Jesus have faced Calvary without feeling discouraged?

What might have been the result if Jesus would have become discouraged and fainthearted while facing Calvary?

Today let's look at a few verses dealing with the importance of having **joy** in our lives. Drink deeply from God's promises!

Isaiah 12:3. *"With joy you will drink deeply from the fountain of salvation!"* (NLT)

Jeremiah 15:16. *"Your words are what sustain me. They bring me great joy and are my heart's delight, for I bear your name, O LORD God Almighty."* (NLT)

Luke 6:22,23. *"God blesses you who are hated and excluded and mocked and cursed because you are identified with me, the Son of Man. When that happens, rejoice! Yes, leap for joy! For a great reward awaits you in heaven."* (NLT)

2 Cor 1:24. *"We want to work together with you so you will be full of joy as you stand firm in your faith."* (NLT)

1 Thess. 1:6. *"So you received the message with joy from the Holy Spirit in spite of the severe suffering it brought you. In this way, you imitated both us and the Lord."* (NLT)

1 Peter 1:8. *"You love him even though you have never seen him. Though you do not see him, you trust him; and even now you are happy with a glorious, inexpressible joy."* (NLT)

1 Peter 4:13. *"Instead, be very glad--because these trials will make you partners with Christ in his suffering, and afterward you will have the wonderful joy of sharing his glory when it is displayed to all the world."* (NLT)

Remember that it is Yah Shua's **humility and gentleness** that secures this **joy**.

19

Daily Prayer:

Dear Father,
Help me this day to delight in Your Word and the promises You have make.

How is God's Word like a fountain?

How can a person rejoice when facing trials?

Do you ever experience joy from the Holy Spirit?

How does going through trials make us partners with Christ?

VICTORIOUS PRAYER FOR JOY

Oh, Father, I thank you for the **joy** that comes through knowing you. Continue your good work of developing Yah Shua's Yoke in my life. Help me to greet each person you bring my way with **humility and gentleness.** I face many trials but I believe you will use each one to teach me to trust you more than ever before in my life. I am your child. I rejoice in having you for my Father. I trust you completely. I love you, Father. I pray in Yah Shua. Amen.

TRUST FOR JOY

- **T.** Father, I thank you for the **TEST** that you have allowed to come into my life. This trial makes me feel discouraged and defeated, but I thank you in faith that You are working in my life.
- **R.** Father, I now **REPENT** of my desire to feel defeated and depressed. Please forgive me for not trusting in you before I focus on myself.
- **U.** Father, I thank you for your **UNDERSTANDING** you are going to bring into my life through this trial. I thank you that I am going to learn more of you as I allow you to work in this situation.
- **S.** I will **SANCTIFY** my life by meditating on the verse that says I should count it a joy to go through this trial for your glory. **James 1:2-3** *"Dear brothers and sisters, whenever trouble comes your way, let it be an opportunity for joy. For when your faith is tested, your endurance has a chance to grow."* (NLT)
- **T.** I will **TRIUMPH** in how you are working in me, giving me your **joy** in this **test** by sharing this with my Yokefellow.

Daily Prayer:

Dear Father,
Restore to me this day the joy of my salvation.

As we pray today we will be praying in faith that God's will is to give to us His joy.

Be able to share the TRUST_strategy today from memory with your Yokefellow.

Memorize and meditate on James 1:2-3 if you have not already done so.

Thank God for the humility and gentleness He is building into your character.

> **Live what you are learning!**

Yah Shua Yoke #2: WISDOM

James 1:5
If you need __wisdom__--if you want to know what God wants you to do--ask him, and he will gladly tell you. He will not resent your asking. (NLT)

I have become convinced that **wisdom is a character quality** more than it means being intelligent! I believe it is part of Yah Shua's Yoke for all of our lives as Christians. As we see in this verse, **wisdom is something only God can give to us**! Let's take a journey back to when God asked the newly crowned King Solomon to ask for anything Solomon wanted and He would give it. What a great offer from God! Do you remember what Solomon asked for? He asked simply for God to give him wisdom! In 1 Kings 3 is where this dramatic event occurred as well as in Chronicles. In other words the same event is recorded in both books. In the Chronicles account the word wisdom is used; but in the account in 1 Kings, Solomon uses a very vital phrase for wisdom which is thrilling to see. Take a look with me!

1 Kings 3:9
"Give therefore thy servant an *__understanding heart__* to judge thy people, that I may discern between good and bad: for who is able to judge this thy so great a people?" (KJV)

An **understanding heart** is God's definition for **wisdom**! Now we ask, what is an understanding heart? Let's take a look at the meaning of the word translated **understanding** here and the glory of Yah Shua's Yoke will start to become vividly clear!

UNDERSTANDING: To hear intelligently often with implication of attention, attentively, consider, diligently, discern, give ear, (cause to, let, make to) hear.

Daily Prayer:

Dear Father,
Please help me this day to develop a hearing heart of wisdom for you glory.

How would you define __wisdom__ today?

Is wisdom a sign of mental ability or an attitude of one's heart?

Why would King Solomon ask for wisdom instead of riches or fame?

Why is discernment necessary in order to make godly decisions?

As we saw yesterday, biblical understanding is rooted in **hearing** or listening. To be more specific, Solomon asked for a **Hearing Heart**! The Yah Shua Yoke of wisdom is to ask God to give us a Hearing Heart. If you think about this for just a moment, this is not something that is related to mental intelligence; but wisdom is actually a condition of the heart where God is at work!

When we think about Yah Shua's interactions with people in the gospels we always see His great wisdom. Whether He was talking to the worst of sinners, the desperately ill, or the most arrogant aristocrat, Yah Shua always listened with His heart. Because He listened with His heart, He knew their hearts. When you talk with someone you can tell very quickly if they are talking **at** you or if they are listening **to** you. Wisdom is learning to listen to God's heart with our spirit as we listen to people with our hearts. When we listen with God's heart, friends will leave us refreshed; enemies will leave us perplexed! Look at a few verses on wisdom with our understanding of wisdom being a **Hearing Heart**!

Ephesians 1:17
Asking God, the glorious Father of our Lord Jesus Christ, to give you spiritual wisdom and understanding, so that you might grow in your knowledge of God. (NLT)

1 Kings 10:24
And all the earth sought to Solomon, to hear his wisdom, which God had put in his heart. (NLT)

Proverbs 15:33
The fear of the LORD is the instruction of wisdom; and before honor is humility. (NLT)

Colossians 4:5
Walk in wisdom toward them that are without, redeeming the time. (NLT)

Daily Prayer:

Dear Father,
Give me this day a burning desire to have Your wisdom, Your understanding Heart.

Has your understanding of wisdom changed since yesterday and if so, how has it changed?

Do you naturally listen intently to people or is it a struggle to pay attention?

Ask someone close to you today if they always feel like you pay special attention when they have something to tell you. Who is this person?

What was their answer?

TRUST FOR A HEARING HEART

As we seek a hearing heart it is important to believe that the Father will freely give this wisdom to us. James tells us that God will freely give it, in fact He longs to give it. Let's take a serious look at James' instruction.

James 1:5-8
If you need wisdom--if you want to know what God wants you to do--ask him, and he will gladly tell you. He will not resent your asking. But when you ask him, be sure that you really expect him to answer, for a doubtful mind is as unsettled as a wave of the sea that is driven and tossed by the wind. People like that should not expect to receive anything from the Lord. They can't make up their minds. They waver back and forth in everything they do. (NLT)

As we see here, God wants us to ask for wisdom; but He also wants us to ask in TRUST, believing that we will receive it. To not TRUST God to give wisdom when we ask is the same as being two different people at the same time. God does not want us doubting Him or His Word. When we TRUST God, we bring great joy to His heart. When we doubt God, we insult His character. Now I feel certain that none of us have ever intentionally set out to insult God, but we must grow in our understanding that when we doubt Him that is exactly what we do. A lack of faith or TRUST in God will greatly diminish His ability to work in our lives. The goal of God for growing Christians is to bring us to the place where we trust Him more than ourselves. We want the answers now, God wants our TRUST!

Daily Prayer:

Dear Father,
Help me today to see each person I meet as an opportunity to share and express your wisdom.

Where does wisdom come from?

How do we gain wisdom?

Who do you know that needs God's wisdom today?

How would you go about sharing God's wisdom with this person?

Let's apply this knowledge of wisdom to our TRUST model for spiritual growth.

- **T.** I thank you Father for this **TRIAL** you have allowed to come into my life. I rejoice in the knowledge that you are working to increase my spiritual strength. Please give me your **Hearing Heart** in this situation. I believe you will give it to me!

- **R.** Father, I now **REPENT** of my lack of faith in your promise that you will freely give me a hearing heart as your Word says in **James 1:5 "If you need wisdom... ask him, and he will gladly tell you. He will not resent your asking."** (NLT)

- **U.** Father, I thank you for the **UNDERSTANDING** you are going to give me about the way you listen and see this trial.

- **S.** Father, I will **SANCTIFY** my heart by meditating on James where you have promised to give your gift of wisdom to me. **James 1:5 "If you need wisdom...ask him, and he will gladly tell you. He will not resent your asking."** (NLT)

- **T.** Thank you for the victory you are giving me, and I am going to **TRIUMPH** in Your work by sharing what you are doing in my life with _____.

Congratulation! You are well on your way to experiencing Yah Shua's Yoke of **wisdom** in your life in ways you never knew before!

James 3:17
But the wisdom that comes from heaven is first of all pure. It is also peace loving, gentle at all times, and willing to yield to others. It is full of mercy and good deeds. It shows no partiality and is always sincere. (NLT)

Daily Prayer:

Dear Father,
Please help me this day to apply the TRUST model to my life from my heart.

Have you started getting accustomed to thanking God for the trials that come your way day to day?

Why would repenting of our natural desires be dependent on having faith in God?

Have you started to sense the Holy Spirit actually changing your heart, giving to you His wisdom? Can you describe this?

Read James 3:17 at the left and examine yourself to see if this accurately describes your relationship to others, especially those closest to you! In what areas do you need to change?

LISTENING WITH OUR HEARTS

Please allow me to add that it is often difficult to listen to people with our hearts. We all by nature are much more interested in being understood ourselves than in taking the time to understand anyone else.

Spouses, do you really take the time to try to understand your life mate? Husbands, would you be willing to take the time to understand the fears of your wives? Wives, do you understand the needs of your husbands? Parents, do you take the time to understand your children? Would you take the time to simply listen to them, to ask God to help you truly understand them?

Church staff person, do you know the precious people God has given to you to serve or do you allow their immaturity to irritate you? On the job, do you listen to your fellow workers? What we find is that people long to be listened to, to be understood. If we would care enough to simply listen, if we would truly care about others, there would be a rich harvest reaped in our lives. God has promised that He would give us a hearing heart, **His heart**, if we would only ask. Ask, then pay attention with our hearts. You will be blessed by what you discover!

Oh, the rewards for those who long to understand others with the very heart of Yah Shua! Oh, the blessings received by those who find someone who will hear them and know them with the heart of God! Oh, the healing of fractured lives that will come!

Will you be that heart of wisdom?

Daily Prayer:

Dear Father,
In faith I ask You for Your hearing heart. Thank you for doing Your good work of wisdom in my life!

Often those closest to us are the most difficult to listen to, why is this so?

What is the link between listening and understanding?

Ask your Yokefellow to share with you something they are struggling with in their life right now. Ask God to help you listen with your heart.

> **Ask your Yokefellow to give you a personal and truthful evaluation of where they think you are right now in becoming a disciple of Christ and write a brief evaluation here.**

Yah Shua Yoke #3: A BRIDLED TONGUE

Do you remember the childhood taunt about hurtful words?

**Sticks and stones
May break my bones,
But Words can never hurt me!**

There has probably never been a statement **less true** ever made! The truth is that words can often cause some of the greatest damage in life! Hurt feelings are much more difficult to heal and mend than actual physical wounds ever will be. And the heart breaking truth is that we will often hurt with words the ones closest to us in life long before we would think of verbally blasting a total stranger. Talk about a mixed up fallen human nature, we have one!

Today, let's start the ultimate challenge, learning to control the **TONGUE**! In James chapter 1 we continue our journey.

James 1:19
Wherefore, my beloved brethren, let every man be swift to hear, slow to speak, slow to wrath. (KJV)

Notice God says first to be swift to hear, and remember that is wisdom, or a hearing heart. Joining wisdom now the Lord says to be **slow to speak**; and you thought that listening was difficult! We are going to be studying what James says about the tremendous **power of the tongue**. Anything of power can be used for good or bad. We can use a hammer to build up or to tear down, for example. We will see that the **tongue** is a lot more powerful than any hammer!

Daily Prayer:

*Dear Father,
Please help me this day to begin to learn the power of a bridled tongue.*

Why would children or adults think that words would not hurt them?

When you think of hurtful things that have been said to you in the past does it ever bring up past emotions? What are those emotions?

Can you identify the Yah Shua Yokes in James 1:19?

What is more useful or hurtful, a hammer or the person using the hammer?

Today consider the amazing claim made by God in James chapter three concerning this member of our bodies, the **tongue**!

James 3:2-16 "We all make many mistakes, but those who control their **tongues** can also control themselves in every other way.

3 We can make a large horse turn around and go wherever we want by means of a small bit in its mouth.

4 And a tiny rudder makes a huge ship turn wherever the pilot wants it to go, even though the winds are strong.

5 So also, the **tongue** is a small thing, but what enormous damage **it** can do. A tiny spark can set a great forest on fire.

6 And the **tongue** is a flame of fire. **It** is full of wickedness that can ruin your whole life. **It** can turn the entire course of your life into a blazing flame of destruction, for **it** is set on fire by hell itself.

7 People can tame all kinds of animals and birds and reptiles and fish,

8 but no one can tame the **tongue**. **It** is an uncontrollable evil, full of deadly poison.

9 Sometimes **it** praises our Lord and Father, and sometimes **it** breaks out into curses against those who have been made in the image of God.

10 And so blessing and cursing come pouring out of the same **mouth**. Surely, my brothers and sisters, this is not right!

11 Does a spring of water bubble out with both fresh water and bitter water?

12 Can you pick olives from a fig tree or figs from a grapevine? No, and you can't draw fresh water from a salty pool.

13 If you are wise and understand God's ways, live a life of steady goodness so that only good deeds will pour forth. And if you don't brag about the good you do, then you will be truly wise!

14 But if you are bitterly jealous and there is selfish ambition in your hearts, don't brag about being wise. That is the worst kind of lie. For jealousy and selfishness

Daily Prayer:

Dear Father,
Please impress upon me the message of James 3 today.

What have you thought about the power of the tongue?

In verse 6 James compares the tongue to the flames of hell itself! What are hell's flames like in your mind?

Notice in verse 10 that the tongue has the power to either bless or to curse. How can we use our tongues to bless?

Verse 14 teaches that the tongue can be motivated by the Devil himself! Have you ever thought of hurtful words as being used by the Devil? Why would James say this?

are not God's kind of wisdom. Such things are earthly, unspiritual, and motivated by the **Devil**.

15 For wherever there is jealousy and selfish ambition, there you will find disorder and every kind of evil.

16 But the wisdom that comes from heaven is first of all pure. It is also peace loving, gentle at all times, and willing to yield to others. It is full of mercy and good deeds. It shows no partiality and is always sincere." (NLT)

Wow! What a graphic description of the **TONGUE** we saw yesterday! But there is hope!

Please note the tremendous promise given is verse #2. We will look first at the New Living Translation's then the King James Version's reading of this verse.

James 3:2 **"We all make many mistakes, but those who _control their tongues_ can also control themselves in every other way."** (NLT)

James 3:2 **"For in many things we offend all. If any man offend not in word, the same is a perfect man, and able also to bridle the whole body."** (KJV)

Did you catch the promise? God says that if a person can get their **tongue** under the control of His Holy Spirit that person will be **fully mature** in every way! Let's take another look at verse eight!

James 3:8
But no one can _tame the tongue_. _It_ is an uncontrollable evil, full of deadly poison. (NLT)

The point here is that we cannot tame the tongue ourselves, we need God's help. We need the power of the Holy Spirit. We need Yah Shua's Yoke of a **Bridled Tongue**. I want to encourage you to read through the entire book of James right now and pay special attention to the emphasis on the tongue throughout the whole book. As the gravity of the tongue soaks into our minds and hearts, it will become abundantly clear why God places so much importance on this one little member of our bodies. Again, do you want to be a mature disciple of Yah Shua? **Learn to trust God to bridle your tongue** and to bring it under the power of the Holy Spirit.

Daily Prayer:

Dear Father,
Help me to apply the promise given by Your Word about the proper use of the tongue.

What is the promise given in James 3:2?

Have you ever made a decision to try to become spiritually mature and failed?

Are you ready to strive for full maturity?

What power does it take to control the tongue?

How many chapters in James speak directly about the tongue?

How serious should we be about controlling the tongue?

TRUST AND THE TONGUE

T. I thank you Father for the **TRIALS** you are going to allow to come into my life that are going to teach me to depend on you to bridle my tongue.

R. As the tests come I am going to be tempted to run my mouth like some baby controlled only by my own personal desires and demands. I now **REPENT** of my sinful nature's desire to strike out and injure another with my tongue. I now **REPENT** of my desire to be heard and show how smart I am and how preferred over others I want to be at the expense of their spiritual well being.

U. I thank you for the **UNDERSTANDING** you are giving about how wonderful it is to be truly controlled by your Spirit! I thank you for the spiritual strength and character you are building into my life. I thank you for making me like Yah Shua, who when reviled, opened not His mouth. I thank you that I am learning to care only for your admiration, not any other person or group in the whole world!

S. I am so grateful for James 3:2, and the promise of full maturity it gives, *"We all make many mistakes, but those who control their tongues can also control themselves in every other way."* (NLT) I will **SANCTIFY** my mind and heart meditating on this verse and others you reveal that I need in my heart.

T. I will **TRIUMPH** and share with my Yokefellow what You are doing in my life for Your great glory.

Daily Prayer:

Dear Father,
Help me to embrace my trials instead of running from them today.

What is a current test you are going through?

What does you human nature want to do?

How is your understanding of God's ways growing?

Write James 3:2 from memory. How is God's Spirit using this verse to sanctify your thoughts?

Speak words of blessing to your Yokefellow and several family members today!

Please remember that bridling the tongue is a life long pursuit!

We must live in TRUST moment by moment each day of our lives. The good news is that the longer we receive the Spirit's victory by yielding to Him (**humility and gentleness**), the more **natural** our spiritual responses will become as we take on Yah Shua's Yoke. There is great **joy** in having our words used by the Spirit for God's great good through our humility.

Just as we have seen that the tongue can be used for great harm, it can also be used for great good! Raising children with not only food, clothing, and a wonderful house, but also loving, building, affirming words are just as important! The power to transform a marriage partner by building them up with loving words of kindness and understanding is vital to healthy relationships! These are ways that the tongue can turn a house into a home.

In the church, words are all-important. Even spiritual gifts can be abused just like the hammer can be abused. Look at this verse from Paul's letter to Corinth:

1 Cor. 14:3
But one who prophesies is helping others grow in the Lord, encouraging and comforting them. (NLT)

How many of us have known those claiming to have a prophetic gift use words to expose and hurt others instead of building and encouraging? When used properly, the tongue under the Spirit's control becomes a source of life-giving power from God Himself!

Daily Prayer:

Dear Father,
I commit to You from this day forward my tongue as Your vessel for Your service alone.

Can we ever take a break from yielding our tongue to God's Spirit?

How do humility and gentleness have any effect on how we use our tongues?

If you have used your tongue to hurt those close to you please ask forgiveness from them today.

If you have ever used your tongue to hurt others at church or on the job ask their forgiveness today.

Why would asking forgiveness for things we have said make us more likely to want to control our tongues in the future?

Yah Shua Yoke #4: TAMED ANGER

The last Yah Shua Yoke we need to take on (that's right, LAST! I told you this was going to be easy!) is allowing the Spirit to tame our **anger**. Anger is an **emotion**. Emotions are the things we feel. Far too often we allow our emotions to control our actions. One person has said that the person who is controlled by his emotions has a fool in control of his life! (That person was King Solomon by the way. We will see where he says this in a moment.)

Many would tell us that it is wrong to suppress our emotions, but these voices are not speaking from a spiritual standpoint. Now for the poor person who is not a Christian, it is a tragic condition he finds himself in regarding emotions. He doesn't have the Spirit's presence and help in this confusing area of life. For this person to **suppress** emotions means he must live with his emotions without being able to deal with them effectively. His emotions, therefore, build up and accumulate like floodwaters behind a dam. Ultimately something is going to have to give! He will have an emotional break like a dam breaking after too much water builds up, or simply spills over in a destructive flood. The result is either a constant flood of spewing emotions (anger, rage, fear, lust, jealousy, greed, bitterness, etc....) or an all-out emotional breakdown. The disciple of Yah Shua has a better way of dealing with the same emotions, the Holy Spirit's power!

James 1:19-20
Dear friends, be quick to listen, slow to speak, and _slow to get angry_. Your anger can never make things right in God's sight. (NLT)

32

Daily Prayer:

Dear Father,
Help me to be strong this week in learning to yield my emotions to You for Your use alone.

Go back to day 1 of week 1 and record what you recorded as the thing that makes you the angriest.

Ask God to teach you how to spiritually deal with this anger this week.

Have you ever been told it was wrong to suppress your emotions?

Have you ever used anger to force your way? What was the result?

Was it worth it in the long run?

I believe that if we can **yield our anger** to the Lord's power, then we will be able to yield all negative emotions to the Spirit's control. (**Many emotions are positive**. All positive emotions grow out of the one true great emotion of **love**: compassion, mercy, kindness, gentleness, goodness, etc.)

James states in verse 20 that anger cannot make things right in God's sight. Our vented anger will never produce a godly result. What the Spirit does is to take our yielded emotion of anger and convert it into His Spirit's good **burden of concern** about the person or situation we feel anger toward! What did the Apostle Paul feel over his own peoples' rejection of Christ? I'm sure he felt anger, hurt, rejection, etc., but he yielded all those natural feelings to the Spirit and the result was compassion! As a matter of fact, Paul said he was so burdened over the Jews that he would be willing to be rejected by Christ Himself if only the Jews would accept Christ! What a great transformation of the human heart!

Proverbs 12:16
"A _fool is quick-tempered_, but a wise person stays calm when insulted." (NLT) (Remember we said we were going to see where Solomon said this!)

Matthew 5:22
"But I say, _if you are angry_ with someone, you are subject to judgment! If you say to your friend, 'You idiot,' you are in danger of being brought before the court. And if you curse someone, you are in danger of the fires of hell." (NLT)

Ephesians 4:26, 27
And _don't sin by letting anger gain control over you_. Don't let the sun go down while you are still angry, for _anger gives a mighty foothold to the Devil_. (NLT)

Daily Prayer:

Dear Father,
Help me to be motivated by the great emotions that come with Your love in my life.

What happens when we allow God to take our negative emotions?

What are some negative emotions you struggle with?

What would be the positive emotions God could transform the negative emotions into?

What is a quick-tempered person referred to in Proverbs 12:16?

Jesus in Matthew 5:22 says that anger can make us subject to what?

How does anger give the Devil a foothold in our life?

One fellow believer struggled constantly with anger toward things that a close relative had done toward another close relative. This was a tremendous trial for this sister in Christ. Her anger often left her depressed, hurt, crying, and growing more bitter by the day. She often found herself talking negatively about the relative and afterward compounding her emotional pain by then feeling more and more guilty for responding so harshly! She knew she needed to change but did not know how. One day while working through the TRUST strategy God revealed to her what she was doing and how much she was hurting herself by allowing her emotions to have such control in her life. She began repenting of her desired response, calling it sin, and asked for God's wisdom and help. God came through! Suddenly she started seeing her relative through God's eyes! She felt God's compassion and concern for her relative. Suddenly the Spirit flooded her heart with a genuine burden for the offending relative! Her life has been transformed by the Spirit's power as she has taken on Yah Shua's Yoke in her heart. **The result has been peace in her heart!**

What every human longs for more than anything is **rest** in their hearts! Billions of people are looking to a large variety of activities, pleasures, things, religion, or people to find this rest. Bless their hearts, rest is never found outside of Yah Shua's Yoke. Many Christians are also looking to wrong things to find this rest. Even though they are children of God, even though they have tried all types of church service, church activities, and church work, they still feel that something is missing. What is missing is Yah Shua's character of **humility and gentleness** which is only acquired through Yah Shua's Yoke.

Daily Prayer:

Dear Father,
Please help me to depend on Your Spirit to control the anger in my life.

Have you ever struggled with anger and hurt like the lady in this example?

How did you deal with the problem?

What were the results?

What might God have done if He had been allowed to be in control of your emotions?

Would you describe your life as having an abundance of inner peace?

Would you be willing now to apply the TRUST model to the emotional trials in your life?

TRUST

- **T.** Father, I thank you for the **TRIAL** you have allowed to come into my life. I want to pass this test by your grace and for your glory alone.
- **R.** Father, I now **REPENT** of my desired response of anger. I have been hurt. I need your help to tame my feelings and bring them under your control. Please forgive me for wanting to seek revenge in my own way, in my own time. I yield my heart and feelings to you.
- **U.** I thank you for the **UNDERSTANDING** you are going to bring into my life as a result of this test. Understanding your ways is more important to me than getting my way.
- **S.** I will allow Your Spirit to **SANCTIFY** my heart by meditating on **James 1:20** that says, *"Your anger can never make things right in God's sight."* (NLT)
- **T.** I will **TRIUMPH** in the victory you give to me by sharing this with my Yokefellow.

Daily Prayer:

Dear Father,
Help me to learn to trust You more in every area of my life for Your glory.

What is a trial you are going through right now that makes you want to be angry?

What does your anger make you want to do?

Have you ever lost sleep because of being angry?

Are you now experiencing victory over anger?

Describe that victory to your Yokefellow!

A NEW BEGINNING

Matthew 11:28-30

Then Jesus said, "Come to me, all of you who are weary and carry heavy burdens, and I will give you <u>rest.</u> Take my yoke upon you. Let me teach you, because I am <u>humble and gentle</u>, and you will find <u>rest</u> for your souls. For my yoke fits perfectly, and the burden I give you is light." (NLT)

Rest is the product of Yah Shua's Yoke. The Holy Spirit will never allow our good works or our **self-effort** to satisfy this longing in the human heart. As we learn to TRUST in the Father to work in our lives, to work through difficult situations, and to transform our hearts to His heart, we learn to rest in Him. This is **humility**. This is **gentleness**. The Father through our presence will bless people who know us. People will actually see a demonstration of God's grace at work in our daily living. People will receive God's grace through our lives. This is true not only of the big tests but also the **small** tests. For example, **every conversation** we have is a test of Yah Shua's character in our lives!

To be known by our Father as a person who is filled with joy, one who listens with a hearing heart, one who has a bridled tongue, and tamed anger in the face of all of life's twists, is God's greatest goal for our lives. This is a description of your life in Christ!

Are you ready to begin? The TRUST strategy is just a simple tool. Like any other tool, it is only effective if put into use. It is free for the taking. The rewards are worth more than anything life has to offer. God's offer is Yah Shua's Yoke.

Daily Prayer:

Dear Father,
I look forward to an abundant life filled with Your presence and power through Your Holy Spirit as I live in Yah Shau's Yoke.

How has Jesus started to take on a new reality in your life?

You have worked hard to get to this place in the "Disciple Yokes" journey! As you apply the things you have learned you will know beyond a doubt that you are walking with Christ!

Joy, wisdom, a bridled tongue and tamed anger are the new qualities of your life!

Enter your personal prayer and desire to God our Father here.

Dear Father, make us one as you and Yah Shua are one.

James 1:2-4
"Dear brothers and sisters, whenever trouble comes your way, let it be an opportunity for joy. For when your faith is tested, your endurance has a chance to grow. So let it grow, for when your endurance is fully developed, you will be strong in character and ready for anything." (NLT)

May God give His richest blessings to you on this, the greatest journey.

If you would like to contact us about how God is working in your life or have any questions you may do so at:

Disciple Yokes
C/O Cedar Heights Church
14502 Cedar Heights Rd.
NLR, AR 72118

Or e-mail Chuck at:
achuckels@yahoo.com

We would love to hear from you!

Make a list here of three people you would like to see learn to become a disciple of Yah Shua.

1)

2)

3)

Begin to pray daily for them.

Ask God to bless them.

Be spiritual salt and light in their lives.

Call them weekly to see how they are doing.

Share with them what Disciple Yokes has done for you.

Offer to be their Yokefellow or offer to help them find a <u>Disciple Yokes</u> group.

THE LETTER OF YA'AKOB

(Translated from the original Greek by Dr. Robert Michael Head, used by permission.)

1:1 Ya'akob,[1] slave of God and of the Lord Yah Shua the Messiah[2]. To the twelve tribes scattered:
>> Greetings.

2 When you are involved in various tests, my brothers and sisters,
> <u>let it be</u>[3] a joyful* experience,

3 knowing that these tests of your faith
>> produce unending endurance.

4 In addition, <u>you must have</u> the total fulfillment
> that comes from that same unending endurance,
>> even the wholeness* that comes
>>> from lacking nothing.

5 But if any of you lacks wisdom,*
> <u>you must ask</u> of God,
>> who gives bountifully
>> (and not reluctantly),
> and He will give it to you.

6 But <u>you must ask</u> in faith*
> without doubt: for the doubter is like a wave of the sea, agitated by the wind and tossed about.

7 However, <u>do not think</u> a person like that
> will receive anything from Yahweh;[4]

> *Joy is the first Yoke to apply to life.*

> *Wisdom is a hearing heart.*

> *Faith is learning to TRUST God.*

---

[1] Formerly called "James." The Greek accurately uses the name Ιακωβοθ...Jacob or Ya'akob.

[2] Ξριστοθ, or "Christ," is a Greek translation of the word "Messiah." It is not our Savior's name, but His title.

[3] All words in the Greek command tense (imperative) are underlined.

[4] Jews became afraid of speaking the name of God, replacing it with other words. Therefore, we end up with statements like this: "His name is the LORD." His name is not "LORD," but Yahweh (as is reflected in the Hebrew text of the Old Testament). We have attempted to restore this gift to God's people in this translation.

8 he is a man trying to lead two lives,[5]
    unstable in all his ways.

9 The humble person on one hand
    must glory in his high position,

10 but the distinguished person must glory in his humble* position, because like a flower of the field
    he will pass away.

11 For the sun rises with the scorching wind
    and the field (even its' flowers)
    will come to an end;
in the same way, the fame of the popular
    will be absolutely destroyed.

12 Blessed is the person who patiently endures a test,*
because when he passes through a test successfully
    he will receive the crown of life
      promised to those who love God.[6]

13 But the one who is attracted to sin[7] must not say,
"God is the source of my attraction":
For God is not tempted by evil,
and He leads no one into temptation.*

14 But each one is attracted by the seducing and entrapment
    of his own desire:

15   when that same desire conceives
      it births sin,
        but when sin is fully mature
        it brings death.

16 <u>Do not wander off course</u>,[8]
    my beloved brothers and sisters,

Humility is the basis of Yah Shua's character.

Tests will come, we don't have to search for them!

Temptation is the result of our human nature's desired response, as opposed to experiencing God's purpose through TRUST.

---

[5] Traditionally rendered "double-minded," the Greek word δίψυξοδ (di'-psoo-kos) is more accurately understood as "double-lived." In Mark 3:21, Yah Shua's relatives say of Him (literally), "He is beside Himself." A whole or unified person was seen as spiritually healthy in the Bible. This attitude of completion is a major theme of Ya'akob's letter.

[6] Compare this promise to 2:5.

[7] Ya'akob clarifies his argument: God sends tests and trials, but is NOT the source of the temptations that pull at our affections.

[8] The Greek word for "error" is πλανη (plah'-neh), where we get our English word "planet." While stars have a steady course in the sky, planets appear to suddenly backtrack and wander off-course. Ya'akob appeals to us to be more like the Creator of the heavenly bodies, who is superior to His Creation.

like the planets in heaven that don't seem to follow any path.

17 But all lovely things given and all perfect gifts
> are from above
>> from the Father of Heaven,
>>> who is constant and is never eclipsed.

18 The One who was Appointed[9] created us
> by the Word of truth
>> to be His prized possession out of all Creation.

19 <u>Know this</u>, my beloved brethren:
> Everyone <u>must be</u> quick to listen,*
> slow to speak,** slow to anger:***

20 For the anger of man
> will never accomplish God's will.[10]

21 Therefore in gentleness lay aside* all
> filthiness and leftover malice,
<u>Receive</u>* the implanted Word
> which is able to save your lives.

22 But <u>be</u> doers of the Word*
> and not hearers only
>> (who, not applying on what they hear convince themselves of untruth).

23 Because if anyone is a hearer of the Word and not a doer,*
> this one is like a man
> who observes the face he was born with
> in a mirror:

24 when he observes himself

25 and walks away
>> he immediately forgets
>> the sort of person he was.

25 But the one who gazes intently* at the fulfilled law of freedom[11]
> and continues in it,

Quick to Listen/A Hearing Heart.
**Slow to Speak/A Bridled Tongue.*
***Slow to anger/ Tamed Anger.*

Lay Aside/this is Repentance.
Receive the implanted Word/ this is Sanctification through meditation.
Being a 'Doer' is to learn to 'Triumph' with the TRUST strategy.

Vss. 23&24 describes a lack of repentance.

Gazes Intently/a beautiful picture of meditation.

---

[9] Synonym for the concept "Messiah."

[10] Usually δικαιοσυνη (di-kai-ah-soo'-neh) is translated "righteousness." We have described it as being within God's will. Isn't the rightness, justice, generosity, godliness, and piety described by δικαιοσυνη all part of being united with God's will?

[11] What is this Law? See 2:8.

not becoming a forgetful hearer but a doer of work,

    this one is blessed in all he does.

26   If anyone imagines himself religious

    and has not controlled his tongue*

    but seduces his own heart,

        this man's religion is worthless.

27   The pure and honest religion of our God and Father is this:

    Look out for orphans and widows in their tribulations,

    and keep yourselves untainted by the world.*

2:1* My brothers and sisters,

    it is not in showering attention on popular persons

    that you have the faith of the Lord Yah Shua

        the Messiah of glory.

2   Suppose one of these popular people enters into your congregation,

    a person having rings of gold on his fingers

    wearing the most magnificent clothes.

Then a lowly, humbled man enters in wearing worn-out clothes.

3   If you look upon the one wearing fancy clothes and say,

    "You sit here in the place of honor,"

    and to the humble, lowly person you say,

    "You stand over there or sit in the place of a servant,"

4   haven't you made a distinction among yourselves

    and become judges with evil thoughts?

5   <u>Listen</u>, my beloved brothers and sisters:

    Hasn't God chosen the humble and lowly of the world

    to be rich in faith and heirs of the Kingdom

    which He promised to those who love Him?[12]

6   But you dishonored the humble, lowly man.

Don't the rich and popular put you down

    and drag you into court?

Bridled Tongue.

Vs. 27 is a description of Yah Shua's humility and gentleness.

Vss. 1-10 requires humility.

---

[12] Compare this promise to 1:12.

7   Don't they slander[13] the lovely Name by which you
     are called?

8   If you are fulfilling the law of the King
          according to the Scriptures,
             "Love those around you as you love yourself,"
                you are doing well.

9   But if you only pay attention to the popular,
          your works are sin
          and you are being convicted by the law
             of violating that law.

10   For whoever keeps all the law
          but makes a mistake concerning even one part,
     becomes guilty of all.

11   The same One who said, "Do not commit adultery,"
          also said, "Do not murder".
          If you are an adulterer, then you are a murderer,
          becoming a violator of the whole law.

12   In this way speak* and act
          as if you will be judged by the law of freedom.

13   For judgment is without mercy
          for those who don't act mercifully.*
     Mercy is always victorious over judgment.

14* What do you gain, my brothers and sisters,
          if a person says he has faith
             but has no works?
          Is a faith like that able to save him?

15   If a brother or sister is naked
     and lacking food every day

16   but one of your own says to them,
             "Depart in peace, warm yourself and feed
          yourself,"
          but do not give to them what is necessary for
     the body,
             how does that benefit them?

17   Faith is the same way:
          if it doesn't have works,
          it is dead by itself.

18   But someone will say,
          "You have faith, and I have works.
             Show me your faith 'without' works,

| *A Bridled Tongue. |

| *Our need for a Hearing Heart. |

| *Vss. 14-26 reveals our need for Yah Shua's Yoke. |

---

13 Literally, "blaspheme," a word transliterated from the Greek.

and I will show my faith out 'of' works."

19   You believe that God is one, and you do well to believe this:

      the demons also believe* and shudder.

20   But are you willing to come to the realization, you empty-headed person,

      that faith without works is useless?

21   Wasn't Abraham our father made right with God out of works

      when he offered up Isaac his son on the altar?

22   You see that faith together with his works

      (and it was out of works that faith was completed),

23   also fulfilled the Scripture saying,

           "But Abraham believed God,
      and he was considered to be in the will with God",
           and he was called the friend of God.

24   Pay attention to this:
      Out of works a person is put in the will of God
           and not out of faith alone.

25   But in the same way wasn't Rahab the prostitute also put in the will of God out of works

      when she received the messengers and sent them out a different way?

26   For just as the body is dead without the spirit,
      in the same way faith without works is dead.

3:1   Don't let there be many teachers,
      my brothers and sisters,

           seeing that those who are knowledgeable
           will receive a greater judgment upon failure.

2   If anyone does not stumble in the what he says,*

           this complete man is able to control his whole body.

3   Now if we put a bridle in a horse's mouth
      to control him,

           we also lead the whole body.

4   And look at large ships as well,

           even though they are driven by strong winds,

                they are directed by a small rudder
      wherever the pilot wants.

*Demons 'believe' but will not repent.

*Vss. 1-12
A graphic description of our need for a bridled tongue!

44

5   In the same way the tongue, though it is a small part of the body,

    brags about great things.

    See how the smallest flame sets fire to a great forest!

6   And the tongue is a fire like that; the world without God's will!

        The tongue is part of our body,

            the part that makes our whole body filthy,

            sets fire to the plans of our lives,

            and burns with the fire of Hell itself!

7   For every kind of wild animal and bird and reptile and sea life

        is kept in its place and has always been kept in its place by humanity,

8   but no one has been able to tame the tongue of man.

        It is evil and unstable,

        full of deadly venom.

9   With the tongue we bless Yahweh,

        who is also our Father,

    and with the tongue we curse men

        who have been made in the image of God.

10 Out of the mouth comes blessing and cursing.

    There is no need, my brothers and sisters,

        for it to be this way.

11 Does a fountain produce both sweet and bitter water?

12 Can a fig tree, my brothers and sisters, produce olives,

        or an olive tree produce figs? Of course not!

        Neither can salt water produce fresh water.

13 Who has discernment and understanding among you?

        Let this person prove it through his or her good conduct and speech

            which come out of a gentle wisdom.*

14 But if you have bitter jealousy and selfish ambition* in your heart,

            do not act as if you are in authority over others

            and do not deceive by perverting the truth.

15   This type of "wisdom" is not divinely inspired,

A Hearing Heart.

UNTamed Anger.

but is lowly,

is the instinct of the unsaved,

and is demonic in nature.

16 For wherever there is jealousy and selfish ambition,

there is chaos and every kind of evil imaginable.

17 But wisdom* from above is first pure,

then peaceful, gentle, encouraging of good relationships,

full of mercy, and producing good things in our lives, steady without hypocrisy.

18 Now the results of a life in the will of God

are produced in peace by those who desire peace.

4:1* Where does this struggle against each other come from?

How about the constant arguments and debates?

Doesn't it come from the tendency still within you

to act as a lost person does?

2 You want what you don't have,

so you destroy it.

You are envious of what others have,

so you ruin your relationship with them.

You do not have because you do not ask.

3 You ask and do not receive,

because you ask with a wrong focus,

desiring to waste everything

for the sake of your unsaved desires.

4 Adulterers, don't you know that loving the world

destroys your relationship with God?

Therefore anyone who chooses to be a friend of the world

puts himself in the position of being the enemy of God.

5 Or maybe you think that this Scriptural principle is meaningless:

"He has a jealous heart for the spirit
He created within us."

6 His heart is revealed in His greatest creation: grace.

That's why Proverbs 3:34 says:

*A wonderful description of a Hearing Heart.

*Vss. 1-5
How untamed anger and a lack of repentance work in our lives!

"God is the enemy of the proud.
                        But He gives grace to
*the humble in spirit."**

7   Because of this: <u>Obey</u> God.
                <u>Resist</u> the Accuser;
                        he will run from you.

8*   <u>Draw near</u> to God;
                        He will draw near to you.
                <u>Make</u> your actions pure, sinners.
                <u>Devote</u> your hearts solely to God,
                        you who are trying to live two
                lives.

9*   <u>Endure</u> difficult work and hard
                times,
                <u>mourn</u>,
                <u>weep</u>.
                <u>Let</u> your laughter be turned to
                mourning,
                        your joy be turned to
                weeping.

10   <u>Humble</u> yourselves before the face
                of Yahweh
                        and He will lift you up.

11*   <u>Do not slander</u> each other, brothers
                and sisters.
                        The one who slanders a
                        brother or sister
                                slanders and judges
                                God's Law.
                But if you judge God's Law,
                you do not fulfill that Law
                but lift up yourself above God's Law
                                        as its' judge.

12   There is one Lawgiver and Judge,
        the same One who saves and destroys:
        Who are you to judge those around you?

13   <u>Listen</u>, those of you who say,
                        "Today or tomorrow we will
                        go to this place,
                        stay a year, do some **business**,
                        turn a profit."

*Yah Shua's Yoke of Humility results in God's Grace poured out in our lives!

*Vs. 8 describes Sanctification.

*Vss. 9&10 describe Repentance.

***Vss. 11-17
A Bridled Tongue.**

14 You don't know what tomorrow will bring to your lives!

For you are like a fog that dissipates before the morning is over.

15 Here's a better saying:
"If Yahweh wills it,
we will live and do
the things of life."

16 The way it is now, though,
you brag about your pride:
this bragging is evil.

17 Therefore knowing God's desire for our lives and not doing it is sin.

5:1* Listen, those of you who are distinguished or popular, weep and cry out to God over the rough times coming to you.

2 Your possessions have rotted
and your fancy clothes have become moth-eaten;

3 your valuables have become rust
and that rust testifies against you
and will consume all that is unsaved in you like a fire.

You have become materialistic in the last days!

4 Look! You have unfairly withheld
the paycheck of those who worked in your fields.

They cry out and the protests of those harvesters
have reached the ear of Yahweh, the **One** who gives rest.

5 You've led a spoiled life here on earth,
gratifying every pleasure and whim.
You have engorged yourself on the desire of your hearts
just as livestock is fattened for the day of slaughter.

6 You have sentenced the man who is in the will of God
(and his way of life)
to death,
and he does not fight you.

Vss. 1-6 Need for Repentance.

48

7   Wait patiently,* brothers and sisters, for the coming of Yahweh.

Look! The farmer waits for the produce of the earth,

patient while it soaks in the rain
of the wet season.

8   You should wait patiently, too,
strengthening* your hearts,
because the coming of Yahweh is near.

9   Don't gripe, brothers and sisters, at one another:

that way you won't be subject to judgment.

Look! The Judge is standing at the door.

10   Brothers and sisters, if you need examples
of the patient waiting and endurance I am talking about,
model yourselves after the prophets
who spoke in the name of Yahweh.

11   Look! Blessed are those who patiently endure.

You've heard of the patient endurance of Job
and the final result of Yahweh's dealings with him:

Yahweh is full of compassion
and kindness.

12   But above all, my brothers and sisters,

don't act like you are signing a contract with heaven and earth

whenever you make a promise;

keep your promises,

your "yes" meaning yes, and your "no" meaning no.

Don't open yourself up to judgment.*

13   Are any of you going through dark times? Pray.

What should you do in good times? Sing praises.*

14*   What if you are sick?

Call for the leaders of the church,

they must pray over you, anointing you
with oil in the name of Yahweh.

15   The prayer lifted up in faith will save the sick,
and Yahweh will raise this person up.

If he or she has been in a lifestyle of sin,

*Trials come.

The Joy of the Lord is our strength!
Neh. 8:10

Need for a Bridled Tongue.

Joy.

Vss 14-20
Need for a Hearing Heart/ Wisdom.

49

they will be forgiven.

16 Because of this, <u>confess</u> your sins to one another,
   <u>praying</u> for one another
   that you will be healed.
The prayer of the person in the will of God can do
a lot of work.

17 Need an example?
   Elijah was a person
who started out needing God for salvation
   (just like us);
but when he was in the will of God
   his prayer for drought was heard.
It did not rain for three and a half years.

18   When he prayed for rain after this,
         the sky opened up,
      and the earth was full of life again.

19 My brothers and sisters,
      if any of you embraces error instead of truth
      and one of you turns this person around,

20 <u>know</u> that turning a sinner from a life guided by
errors
      saves his life out of death and
         covers a huge amount of sin.